FASTING

THE KEY TO RELEASING GOD'S POWER IN YOUR LIFE

Other Titles by Derek Prince

FASTING

THE KEY TO RELEASING GOD'S POWER IN YOUR LIFE

derek prince

WHITAKER HOUSE

FASTING

Derek Prince Ministries
P. O. Box 19501
Charlotte, NC 28219–9501
www.derekprince.org

ISBN-13: 978-0-88368-258-6
ISBN-10: 0-88368-258-3
Printed in the United States of America
© 1986 by Derek Prince Ministries, International

Whitaker House
1030 Hunt Valley Circle
New Kensington, PA 15068
www.whitakerhouse.com

---

16 17 18 19 20 21 22 **UJ** 14 13 12 11 10 09 08

Contents

Chapter One

The Primary Purpose of Fasting

A lost key to successful Christian living that is found throughout the Bible has been set aside and misplaced by the church of today. That key is fasting.

Fasting, as I would define it, is "voluntarily abstaining from food for spiritual purposes." Sometimes people fast not only from food, but also from water; however, that is the exception rather than the rule. Fasting from food only is exemplified in the fast of Jesus in the wilderness before He began His public ministry. Matthew 4:2 says this:

²And after He had fasted forty days and forty nights, He then became hungry.
(Matthew 4:2 NAS)

Clearly Jesus did not abstain from water for those forty days because anyone who has fasted from water will become thirsty before they become hungry. So the fact that the Scripture does not say, "He became thirsty," but just states, *"He then became hungry,"* indicates that Jesus abstained from food but not from water.

Fasting seems unfamiliar and even frightening to many people, yet this attitude is strange. Fasting was regularly practiced by God's people throughout the Bible. Fasting is also an accepted part of most other major world religions, such as Hinduism, Buddhism, and Islam.

Fasting for Self-Humbling

Primarily, the purpose of fasting is self-humbling. It is a scriptural means ordained by God for us to humble ourselves before Him. Throughout the Bible God requires His people to humble themselves before Him. Many different passages of Scripture emphasize this. Here are four from the New Testament:

> [4]*"Therefore, whoever humbles himself like this child is the greatest in the kingdom of heaven."* (Matthew 18:4 NIV)

> [12]*"For whoever exalts himself will be humbled, and whoever humbles himself will be exalted."* (Matthew 23:12 NIV)

> [10]*Humble yourselves before the Lord, and he will lift you up.* (James 4:10 NIV)

> [6]*Humble yourselves, therefore, under God's mighty hand, that he may lift you up in due time.* (1 Peter 5:6 NIV)

One important feature of all these Scriptures is that the **responsibility to humble ourselves is placed upon us.** We cannot transfer that responsibility to God. To pray, "God, make me humble," is unscriptural, because the reply of God in Scripture is always, *"Humble yourself."*

In the Bible God has revealed to us a specific, practical way to humble ourselves. David reveals that fasting was the way that he employed to humble his soul, or to humble himself:

> [13]*"I humbled my soul with fasting..."*
> *(Psalm 35:13 NAS)*

Consider some historical examples where God's people humbled themselves in this way. First, we read in the book of Ezra about how Ezra is preparing to lead a band of returning Jewish exiles from Babylon back to Jerusalem. They have before them a long, arduous journey through country infested by brigands and occupied by their enemies. They are taking with them their wives and children and the sacred vessels of the temple. They are in desperate need of safe conduct. Ezra had two alternatives: he could appeal to the emperor of Persia for a band of soldiers and horsemen, or he could trust in God. He chose to trust in God and this is what he says:

> [21]There, by the Ahava Canal, I proclaimed a fast, so that we might humble ourselves before our God and ask him for a safe journey for us and our children, with all our possessions.
> [22]I was ashamed to ask the king for soldiers and horsemen to protect us from enemies on the road, because we had told the king, "The good hand of our God is on everyone who looks to him, but his great anger is against all who forsake him."
> [23]So we fasted and petitioned our God about this, and he answered our prayer.
> (Ezra 8:21-23 NIV)

Ezra had two alternatives: one carnal, the other spiritual. He could have resorted to the carnal and asked for a band of soldiers and horsemen. It would not have been sinful, but it would have been on a lower level of faith. But he chose the spiritual alternative. He chose to look to God by invoking God's supernatural help and protection. Ezra and the Israelites with him knew exactly how to do this. It was something they already understood. They fasted and humbled their souls before God. They petitioned God, and God heard them and granted them the safe journey for which they asked.

In 2 Chronicles we read the record of an incident in the history of Judah when Jehoshaphat was king:

> *²Some men came and told Jehoshaphat, "A vast army is coming against you from Edom....It is already in Hazazon Tamar"*
> *(that is, En Gedi).*
> *³Alarmed, Jehoshaphat resolved to inquire of the LORD, and he proclaimed a fast for all Judah.*
> *⁴The people of Judah came together to seek help from the LORD; indeed, they came from every town in Judah to seek him.*
> *(2 Chronicles 20:2-4 NIV)*

Then Jehoshaphat prayed a prayer invoking God's help. In the last verse of that prayer, which is very significant, Jehoshaphat concludes by saying:

> [12]*"O our God, will you not judge them? For we have no power to face this vast army that is attacking us. We do not know what to do, but our eyes are upon you."*
>
> *(2 Chronicles 20:12 NIV)*

Here are the key phrases: *"...we have no power...we do not know what to do..."* So they had to turn to God for supernatural help and they knew the way to turn. They renounced the natural to invoke the supernatural.

For another clear example of the practice of fasting in the Old Testament, we turn to the ordinances for the Day of Atonement, what the Jewish people call Yom Kippur:

> [29]*"And this shall be a permanent statute for you: in the seventh month, on the tenth day of the month, you shall humble your souls, and not do any work, whether the*

*native, or the alien who sojourns among
you;*
[Now, where this translation says, "*you
shall humble your souls,*" another translation says, "*you must deny yourselves,*" and,
alternatively, "*you must fast.*" Then the
passage continues:]
[30] "*for it is on this day that atonement shall
be made for you to cleanse you; you shall
be clean from all your sins before the
LORD.*
[31] *It is to be a sabbath of solemn rest for
you, that you may humble your souls; it is
a permanent statute.*"
                          (Leviticus 16:29–31 NAS)

We know, historically, that for 3,500
years the Jewish people have always ob-
served Yom Kippur, the Day of Atonement,
as a day of fasting. We also have the New
Testament authority for this. A passage in
Acts that describes Paul's journey to Rome
by sea says:

[9] *Much time had been lost, and sailing had
already become dangerous because by now
it was after the Fast.*   *(Acts 27:9 NIV)*

12

"The Fast" mentioned here is the Day of Atonement, which always fell at the end of September or the beginning of October, just when winter was setting in. We see from the New Testament that the Day of Atonement was always celebrated as *"the Fast."* God required His people to humble their souls before Him by collective fasting. That was the appointment, the ordinance, for the Day of Atonement, the most sacred day of the Jewish calendar.

Notice two facts: First, in this case, fasting was man's response to God's provision of forgiveness and cleansing. God provided the ceremony by which the High Priest went into the innermost sanctuary of the temple and made atonement. Second, **that atonement was only effective for those people who accepted it through fasting.**

In other words, God did His part, but man had to do his. This is true in many transactions with God. God does His part, but He expects a response from us. Many times the response that God expects from us is to fast.

God absolutely required fasting of all His people under the old covenant. Anyone who did not fast on the Day of Atonement was to be cut off and was no longer to be a member of God's people. So we see that God attached great importance to fasting as the appointed way for His people to humble themselves before Him and so to qualify for the blessing that He wanted to provide.

Chapter Two

New Testament Examples of Fasting

We have seen that fasting is a lost key, one that is found all through the pages of the Bible. Yet is has been set aside and misplaced by the Christian church.

The primary purpose for fasting, as revealed in the Bible, is self-humbling. Fasting is a scriptural way to humble ourselves. All through the Bible God required His people to humble themselves before Him. God has revealed that a simple, practical way to humble ourselves is through fasting.

We have looked at some historical examples from the Old Testament already: examples of David in Psalms; Ezra and the exiles returning from Babylon; Jehoshaphat and the people of Judah; and the Day of Atonement, when every believing Jew was required to practice fasting.

I believe the essential nature of fasting is renouncing the natural to invoke the supernatural. The most natural thing for us to do is to eat. When we give up eating, we are deliberately turning away from the natural by turning to God and to the supernatural. This has a deep significance.

Fasting in the Life of Jesus

Fasting was also part of the life and ministry of Jesus and of the New Testament church. First of all, the Lord Jesus Himself practiced fasting, as reported in the Gospels:

> [1]*Jesus, full of the Holy Spirit, returned from the Jordan and was led by the Spirit in the desert,*
> [2]*where for forty days he was tempted by the devil. He ate nothing during those days and at the end of them he was hungry.*
> *(Luke 4:1-2 NIV)*

As I explained previously, the words indicate that Jesus abstained from food, but probably drank water.

Before Jesus entered His public ministry, there were two critical experiences through which He passed. The first was when the Holy Spirit descended upon Him, and He was endued with the supernatural power of the Holy Spirit for His ministry. But, Jesus still did not immediately go out and begin to minister.

The second experience was forty days of fasting in the desert. He abstained from food and focused on the spiritual. Apparently, during in that time, He had a direct, person-to-person conflict with Satan.

Through His fasting, He emerged victorious from that first conflict with Satan.

This illustration would seem to indicate that fasting is essential in our lives if we are to be victorious over Satan. If Jesus had to practice fasting for victory, I do not see how any of us can claim to achieve victory without the same practice.

Notice the result of fasting in the life of Jesus. Luke 4:14 states:

> *[14]Jesus returned to Galilee in the power of the Spirit, and news about him spread through the whole countryside.* (NIV)

There is a very significant difference in the two phrases used. When Jesus went into the desert, the Gospel says He was *"full of the Holy Spirit."* But when He returned from the desert after forty days of fasting it says He went *"in the power of the Spirit."* In other words, it is one thing to be full of the Spirit, it is another thing to be in the **power** of the Spirit. From the time of His baptism onwards, the Spirit was there. But it was His fasting that released the power of the Holy Spirit to flow through His life and ministry without hindrance. Again, I believe this is a pattern for us.

Jesus Himself said later in John 14:12:

[12]"Truly, truly, I say to you, he who believes in Me, the works that I do shall he do also; and greater works than these shall he do; because I go to the Father." (NAS)

I want to point out that the works Jesus did began with fasting. If we want to follow in the other works He did, it seems logical to me that we must begin where Jesus began—with fasting.

Jesus also taught His disciples to fast. In the Sermon on the Mount, He said to His disciples:

*¹⁷"But when you fast, put oil on your head
and wash your face,
¹⁸so that it will not be obvious to men that
you are fasting, but only to your Father,
who is unseen; and your Father, who sees
what is done in secret, will reward you."*
(Matthew 6:17–18 NIV)

Jesus promises a reward to those who
practice fasting in the right way and for
the right motives. Notice one very important little word. Jesus said, *"when you
fast,"* He did not say, *"if you fast."* Had He
said *"if,"* He would have left open the
possibility that they might not practice
fasting. But when He said, *"when you
fast,"* He obviously assumed that they
would practice fasting.

The theme of the sixth chapter of
Matthew is three main Christian duties:
giving to the poor, praying, and fasting. In
connection with all three of them, Jesus
uses the same word *"when,"* He never says
"if." In verse 2 He says: *"when you give to
the needy..."* And in verse 17 He says,

"when you fast..." He never left open the option that they would not do these three things. He put giving, praying, and fasting on precisely the same level.

Most Christians would accept without much question that it is our obligation to give and to pray. But on that same basis, it is equally our obligation to fast.

Fasting in the Early Church

Not only was fasting practiced by Jesus, it was practiced by the New Testament church. In Acts 13:1–4, we read about the church at Antioch:

> *[1]Now there were at Antioch, in the church that was there, prophets and teachers: Barnabas, and Simeon who was called Niger, and Lucius of Cyrene, and Manaen who had been brought up with Herod the tetrarch, and Saul.* [Five men are named.] *[2]And while they were ministering to the Lord and fasting, the Holy Spirit said,*

> *"Set apart for Me Barnabas and Saul for
> the work to which I have called them."*
> *³Then, when they had fasted and prayed
> and laid their hands on them, they sent
> them away.*
> *⁴So, being sent out by the Holy Spirit, they
> went down to Seleucia and from there they
> sailed to Cyprus.*   *(Acts 13:1-4 NAS)*

The leaders of the church were minis-
tering to the Lord and fasting together. In
the course of their fasting, they received a
revelation from the Holy Spirit that two of
their number were to be sent out for a
special apostolic ministry. Receiving this
revelation, they did not send them out
immediately, but they again *"fasted and
prayed and laid their hands on them..."*
Then it says of those two men that they
were sent out *"by the Holy Spirit."*

Again we see that fasting transfers us
from the natural to the supernatural.
When the church leaders moved out of the
natural realm through fasting, they had a
supernatural revelation and supernatural

authorization, and the Holy Spirit Himself accepted responsibility for what they did. But the way to this was opened up through their collective fasting.

After Paul and Barnabas had gone out on this ministry, we read what they did when they established their new converts in various cities into proper churches:

> *²³And when they had appointed elders for them in every church, having prayed with fasting, they commended them to the Lord in whom they had believed.*
> *(Acts 14:23 NAS)*

Fasting was not just a single, unusual occurrence. It was practiced regularly by the apostles and taught to their new disciples.

The two main events in the spread of the Gospel in the early church were, first, the sending out of apostles and, second, the establishing of new converts through the appointment of elders. It is tremendously significant that the early church did not do either of these things without first fasting and seeking God's supernatural direction and help. In a certain sense, we can say that the outgrowth and expansion of the early church revolved around collective fasting.

Finally, we want to read the testimony of Paul about his life and ministry, remembering that Paul was one of the two men involved in that incident. In 2 Corinthians 6:4–6, Paul says:

> 4...*in everything commending ourselves as servants of God, in much endurance, in afflictions, in hardships, in distresses,*
> 5*in beatings, in imprisonments, in tumults, in labors, in sleeplessness* [watching], *in hunger* [fasting],
> 6*in purity, in knowledge, in patience, in kindness, in the Holy Spirit, in genuine love...* (*2 Corinthians 6:4-6 NAS*)

Paul here describes various aspects of his character and conduct which marked

himself and his fellow-workers as true
servants of God. Among these were watching (staying awake when you could be
asleep) and fasting (abstaining from food
when you could be eating). Watching and
fasting are in very good company. They are
put side by side with purity, knowledge,
patience, kindness, the Holy Spirit and
genuine love. In other words, they are
presented as part of the total equipment of
a true servant of the Lord Jesus Christ. I
believe that God still views them that way
today. God's provision and God's standards
are still the same as they were for Paul
and for the early church.

Chapter Three

How Fasting Changes Us

Thus far, we have seen that fasting is voluntarily abstaining from food for spiritual purposes. Fasting is a way that God Himself has appointed for His people to humble themselves before Him. Jesus Himself practiced fasting and taught His disciples to do the same. The New Testament church followed the example of their Master. When Jesus spoke about fasting, He did not say, "if you fast," but *when you fast.* He thus put fasting on precisely the same level as giving to the needy and praying.

We want to deal with the mechanics of fasting now by seeing how fasting changes the inner personality. The first thing we need to see with absolute clarity from Scripture is this: **the power that makes the Christian life possible is the Holy Spirit.** No other power can enable us to live the kind of life that God requires of us as Christians. It cannot be done in our own will or in our own strength. It can only be done in dependence on the Holy Spirit. Therefore, the key to successful Christian living is knowing how to release the power of the Holy Spirit in our lives so that we can do the things we could not do in our own strength.

Jesus made this clear to His disciples after the resurrection, before He ever released them to go out into ministry of their own. In Acts 1:8, He said:

> [8]*"But you will receive power when the Holy Spirit comes on you; and you will be my witnesses in Jerusalem, and in all Judea*

and Samaria, and to the ends of the
earth." *(Acts 1:8 NIV)*

He said, in effect, "In order to do what
I've charged you to do, you're going to need
power greater than your own. That power
will come from the Holy Spirit. Don't go
and begin to minister until that power of
the Holy Spirit has come to you."

Compare this with the words of Paul in
Ephesians where he is speaking primarily
about power in prayer:

²⁰*Now to him [God] who is able to do
immeasurably more than all we ask or
imagine, according to his power that is at
work within us...* *(Ephesians 3:20 NIV)*

Paul says what God can do far exceeds
the highest that we could ever think or
imagine, but it depends on His power at
work in us. The extent of what God can do
through us does not depend on our think-
ing or imagining. It depends on His supernatural power being released in us and

29

through us, whether it is in prayer, in preaching or in any form of service. The key is knowing **how** to release the power of the Holy Spirit and become channels or instruments through which He can work without hindrance.

Seeing this, we can move to the next key fact of Scripture. **The old, carnal nature opposes the Holy Spirit.** The very essence and character of the old nature is such that it does not yield to the Holy Spirit. It is in opposition to the Holy Spirit. In the New Testament this carnal nature, what we are by nature before we are transformed by the new birth, is called *"the flesh."* This term does not simply mean the physical body. It is the entire nature that we inherited by descent from our first father, Adam, who was a rebel. In other words, lurking somewhere in every one of us there is a rebel. That is the carnal nature!

In Galatians 5:16–17, Paul says about that carnal nature:

> [16]*But I say, walk by the Spirit* [the Holy Spirit], *and you will not carry out the desire of the flesh.*
> [Each of us is dependent on the Holy Spirit.]
> [17]*For the flesh sets its desire against the Spirit, and the Spirit against the flesh; for these are in opposition to one another, so that you may not do the things that you please.*   (NAS)

That is very clear and very important. The carnal nature is in opposition to the Spirit of God. If we yield to the carnal nature, we are opposing the Spirit of God. If we are going to yield to the Holy Spirit, we must deal with the carnal nature, because as long as the carnal nature controls and operates through us, what we do will be in opposition to the Holy Spirit. This applies not only to our physical desires, but it also applies to what the Bible calls the carnal mind, which is the way the old, carnal, unregenerate nature thinks.

In a powerful verse in Romans, Paul states a truth about the carnal mind:

> 7...*the carnal mind is enmity against God: for it is not subject to the law of God, neither indeed can be.* (Romans 8:7 KJV)

These are strong words Paul is using. He says the flesh opposes the Holy Spirit. He says the fleshly mind is enmity against God. It is not neutrality. There is no suggestion that somehow the carnal nature and the carnal mind can be persuaded to do the will of God. It is impossible. The carnal mind, by its very nature, is enmity against God.

What is the carnal mind? I understand it this way: it is the old, unregenerate soul in its main functions. The functions of the soul are usually defined as will, intelligence and emotions. Each of them can be summed up in a short, familiar, English word. The will says, "I want"; the intelligence (or the mind) says, "I think"; the emotions say, "I feel." Natural, unregenerate man is dominated and controlled by those three expressions of the ego: "I want," "I think," and "I feel." This is the way the carnal nature operates.

If we are to come into submission to the Holy Spirit, and if the Holy Spirit is to operate through us with freedom, then the carnal nature must be brought into subjection to the Holy Spirit. We must subject the "I want," the "I think," and the "I feel" to the Spirit of God. According to God's pattern in Scripture, this is done by fasting. That was how Jesus Himself did it, that was how Paul did it, and that is how you and I are expected to do it.

Here is Paul's own account of how he struggled with his carnal nature and how he gained victory over it. In 1 Corinthians 9:25–27, Paul describes this struggle in

terms of an athlete going into training for
victory in athletics:

> [25]*Everyone who competes in the games* [the
> Olympics] *goes into strict training. They
> do it to get a crown that will not last; but
> we do it to get a crown that will last for-
> ever.*
> [26]*Therefore I do not run like a man run-
> ning aimlessly; I do not fight like a man
> beating the air.*
> [He is saying, "I'm a man with a goal; I'm
> a man with a purpose. I'm a man under
> discipline." And he sums it up this way:]
> [27]*No, I beat my body and make it my slave
> so that after I have preached to others, I
> myself will not be disqualified for the
> prize.*   (1 Corinthians 9:25-27 NIV)

Paul realized that he had to bring his
carnal nature into subjection if he was
going to succeed in his divine calling. This
leaves every one of us with a question:
Which is the master and which is the
servant in each of us? Is the body the
master and the Spirit just the slave? Or is
the Spirit the master and the body the

servant? I will tell you this: **your body makes a wonderful servant, but a terrible master.**

I am reminded of the story of a friend of mine, a lawyer in the Washington, D.C., area, who heard me preach on fasting once and decided it was the right thing to do. He set aside a day to fast and he had a miserable day. Every time he walked out on the street, he seemed to find himself in front of a restaurant where the aroma of cooking was tantalizing or pastries were displayed in the window. He had a tremendous inner struggle to abstain. So, at the end of the day he gave his stomach a "talking-to." He said, "Now, stomach. You've been very rebellious today. You've made a lot of unnecessary trouble for me and for that reason I'm going to punish you. I'm going to fast tomorrow as well as today."

To me that is a tremendous lesson in establishing who is the master and who is the servant. Remember, your body is a wonderful servant, but a terrible master. If you are really going to succeed in the Christian life and win the crown in the "Christian athletics," you are going to have to establish the fact in your own experience that your body does not dictate to you or control you, and that you are not controlled by its whims or appetites. Rather, you must be controlled by a sense of God's divine destiny and purpose for your life. In that regard, you will do everything that is needed to bring your body into subjection so that it does not dictate to you or hinder you in running your race. I believe one of the basic scriptural ways to do this is by the practice of regular fasting.

When you fast, you serve notice on your body and your carnal nature: "You don't control me. I'm not subject to you. You're my servant. You'll obey what the Spirit of God in me declares I have to do."

Chapter Four

Fasting Can Change History

We have seen how fasting changes our inner personalities according to certain principles. First, we must recognize that the power of the Christian life is the Holy Spirit. The Holy Spirit is the only power that will enable anyone to lead a truly Christian life. Second, we must recognize that the flesh, our carnal nature, opposes the Holy Spirit. They are in direct opposition to one another. If the flesh prevails, the Holy Spirit cannot have His way. Third, fasting is God's appointed way to bring the carnal nature into subjection. The Holy Spirit is then free to enable us to do what God desires us to do.

Personally, I believe there is no way to measure the power released by prayer and fasting when practiced with right motives and in accordance with the principles of Scripture. The power thus released can change not only individuals or families, but cities, nations, or even entire civilizations.

I now want to share some examples from the Bible of how fasting has affected the destiny of cities, nations, and empires. Our first example is from the book of Jonah. God called Jonah, the Israelite prophet, to go to Nineveh, a Gentile city and the capital of the Assyrian Empire. Jonah refused to go and tried to run away from God, but God dealt with him very severely. What followed is recorded in the third chapter of Jonah:

> *¹Then the word of the LORD came to Jonah a second time:*
> *²"Go to the great city of Nineveh and proclaim to it the message I give you."*
> *³Jonah obeyed the word of the LORD and went to Nineveh. Now Nineveh was a very*

*important city—a visit required three days
[to go all through it].
⁴On the first day, Jonah started into the
city. He proclaimed: "Forty more days and
Nineveh will be overturned."*

(Jonah 3:1-4 NIV)

Jonah's very simple message was a
final warning of impending judgment on
the city. The response of the Ninevites was
remarkable:

*⁵The Ninevites believed God. They declared
a fast, and all of them, from the greatest to
the least, put on sackcloth [the outward
evidence of mourning].
⁶When the news reached the king of
Nineveh, he rose from his throne, took off
his royal robes, covered himself with sackcloth and sat down in the dust.*

(Jonah 3:5-6 NIV)

Here is a picture of a whole city turning to God in repentance, in fasting, and in
mourning. The proclamation that the king
issued was even more remarkable. It goes
like this:

> [7]*"By decree of the king and his nobles:*
> *Do not let any man or beast, herd*
> *or flock, taste anything; do not let*
> *them eat or drink."*
>
> *(Jonah 3:7 NIV)*

That was a very total fast, not only for the human population but for the livestock; not only did they abstain from food, but also from drinking. And then the proclamation continues:

> [8] *"But let man and beast be covered with sackcloth [again, the outward emblem of mourning]. Let everyone call urgently on God. Let them give up their evil ways and their violence."*
>
> *(Jonah 3:8 NIV)*

This total response is important. Fasting is of no benefit if we continue doing the wrong thing. But it is invaluable as a spiritual help in turning from wrong to do right.

So, the Ninevites not only fasted and covered themselves with sackcloth, they made a proclamation to *"let them give up their evil ways and their violence."* From other passages of Scripture we find that the outstanding sin of Nineveh was violence. Then the proclamation closes this way:

> [9] *"Who knows? God may yet relent and with compassion turn from his fierce anger so that we will not perish."*
>
> [Now here is the divine commentary on this:]
> [10] *When God saw what they did and how they turned from their evil ways, he had compassion and did not bring upon them the destruction he had threatened.*
>
> *(Jonah 3:9–10 NIV)*

You will remember that John the Baptist preached a message of repentance. When certain people came to ask for baptism as evidence of repentance, he said, "I want to see the fruit of repentance in your

41

life. It's no good telling me you've repented if I can't see the results in the way you act." (See Matthew 3:7-8.)

In the case of the Ninevites, God saw how they turned from their evil ways, so He had compassion and did not bring upon them the destruction He had threatened.

It is very interesting to see the historic result. Nineveh was spared for almost two hundred years before it was finally destroyed. During that time in Israel, God had various prophets, such as Amos and Hosea, who brought the message of the warning of judgment and the call to repentance to Israel. Israel had the Scriptures, they had the background of Moses and the Law, and they had the prophets. Many prophets went to the Israelites, but they did not turn.

In contrast, Nineveh had no such background. One prophet went once, and the whole city turned. That is remarkable! It is an interesting consequence that God spared Nineveh and then used the Assyrian Empire, of which Nineveh was the capital, to bring His judgment on Israel!

God's judgment of Israel is a warning, I believe, for Western nations where we have a long background of Christian tradition, knowledge of the Scriptures and the organized church. Could it be that God has been speaking, but we have been as deaf as the people of Israel? Could God send His messengers to some nation with no Christian background so that it would turn to Him, and then use that nation to be an instrument of judgment? Could a nation such as China bring judgment on unrepentant, professing Christian nations? Does that message have an up-to-date application for us?

For a second example of how history was changed by the practice of fasting, we will turn to the book of Esther. The Jewish people were in exile in the Persian Empire, which consisted of 127 provinces covering the known ancient world from Egypt to India. Practically every Jew in the world was living at that time within the confines of the Persian Empire.

A man named Haman had gained great political position and power in the Persian Empire. He persuaded the king to send forth a universal decree for the destruction of all the Jewish people within the confines of his empire on a certain day. This was probably the nearest that anybody has ever come to actually blotting out the Jewish nation—in a sense, even nearer than Adolph Hitler in World War II. It was a crisis such as Israel had never faced in all their history. Their response to this crisis was to turn to God with fasting and prayer.

In particular, Queen Esther (who was Jewish though the king did not know her racial background), set an example which became a pattern for all subsequent generations of the power of prayer and fasting to bring forth intercession that changes history. This is the description in Esther 4:15–17:

> *[15]Then Esther sent this reply to Mordecai:*
> *[16]"Go, gather together all the Jews who are in Susa, and fast for me. Do not eat or drink for three days, night or day. I and my maids will fast as you do. When this is done, I will go to the king, even though it is against the law. And if I perish, I perish."*
> *[17]So Mordecai went away and carried out all of Esther's instructions.* (NIV)

The Jewish people knew what to do. It had been established in the ordinance of the Day of Atonement. They knew the way to humble themselves before God was to fast. All the Jews in the capital city of Susa, from Esther downwards, set aside three days of prayer and fasting. What was the result? In Esther 5:1–3, we read these words:

> *[1]On the third day [of prayer and fasting] Esther put on her royal robes and stood in*

the inner court of the palace, in front of the king's hall. The king was sitting on his royal throne in the hall, facing the entrance.

[2]When he saw Queen Esther standing in the court, he was pleased with her and held out to her the gold scepter that was in his hand. So Esther approached and touched the tip of the scepter.

[3]Then the king asked, "What is it, Queen Esther? What is your request? Even up to half the kingdom, it will be given you."

(Esther 5:1-3 NIV)

Esther went in with her request and changed the entire course of the history of the Persian Empire. Instead of defeat and shame, the situation became honor and promotion for the Jewish people and for their leaders, Mordecai and Esther. The critical turning point was the three-day period when Esther and all the Jews in Susa fasted and sought God. Then their destiny was changed. When Esther went in to the king, he said, "What do you want? It will be given to you up to half the kingdom." In other words, prayer and fasting opened the way for all that Esther could possibly need on behalf of her people.

Esther is a beautiful pattern for us today. God is looking for men and women like Esther who realize the critical nature of our situation and turn to God with their fellow believers in prayer and fasting. Prayer and fasting can still call forth divine intervention on behalf of His people and the critical situation in the world today, just as much as it did in the days of Esther. God is urgently speaking to His people in these days about the need for prayer and fasting.

Chapter Five

Prelude to the Latter Rain

We have seen the measureless power that is released by prayer and fasting when practiced with right motives and in accordance with the principles of Scripture. The power thus released can change not only individuals and families, but whole cities, nations and civilizations. Two historical, biblical examples of this are the city of Nineveh in the time of Jonah, and the Jewish race in the Persian Empire in the time of Esther. In each case, the course of history was radically and permanently changed when a group of people humbled themselves before God by prayer and fasting.

However, we should not look on this kind of history-changing demonstration of God's power as something confined to the past. It is possible, by the same means of prayer and fasting, for us to call forth an intervention of God in history today as powerful and dramatic as those recorded in the Bible. This is both a desperate need and a glorious possibility. In fact, I believe that God is waiting for us to do this.

For an understanding of what God expects from us this way, we turn to the prophet Joel. Joel gives us a brief but comprehensive overview of God's purposes for His people in these last days. Joel opens with a scene of total disaster and desolation. Joel 1:8–12 gives a picture of a desperate and hopeless situation:

8   *Wail like a virgin girded with*
        sackcloth
     For the bridegroom of her youth.
9   *The grain offering and the liba-*
        tion are cut off
     From the house of the LORD.

> The priests mourn,
> The ministers of the LORD.
> 10 The field is ruined,
> The land mourns,
> For the grain is ruined.
> The new wine dries up,
> Fresh oil fails.
> 11 Be ashamed, O farmers,
> Wail, O vinedressers,
> For the wheat and the barley;
> Because the harvest of the field is
> destroyed.
> 12 The vine dries up,
> And the fig tree fails;
> The pomegranate, the palm also,
> and the apple tree,
> All the trees of the field dry up.
> Indeed, rejoicing dries up
> From the sons of men.
>
> *(Joel 1:8-12 NAS)*

The situation is one of desolation, blight, hopelessness, mourning and a total absence of joy. But God then reveals His appointed remedy through the same prophet in the verses that follow. In Joel 1:13–14, God instructs His people:

> [13] *Gird yourselves with sackcloth,*
> *And lament, O priests;*
> *Wail, O ministers of the altar!*
> *Come, spend the night in sack-*
> *cloth,*
> *O ministers of my God,*
> *For the grain offering and the*
> *libation*
> *Are withheld from the house of*
> *your God.*
> [14] *Consecrate a fast,*
> *Proclaim a solemn assembly;*
> *Gather the elders*
> *And all the inhabitants of the*
> *land*
> *To the house of the LORD your*
> *God,*
> *And cry out to the LORD.*
>
> *(Joel 1:13-14 NAS)*

God's remedy is to consecrate a fast and then seek God with desperate prayer. "*Consecrate*" here means to set apart a time for God when you will fast.

God repeats these instructions in Joel 2:12:

¹² "Yet even now," declares the
    LORD,
"Return to Me with all your
    heart,
And with fasting, weeping, and
    mourning."   (Joel 2:12 NAS)

Again, the basic requirement is fasting.
A little further on in Joel, we read:

¹⁵ Blow a trumpet in Zion,
[a public proclamation to all God's people]
    Consecrate a fast, proclaim a
        solemn assembly,
¹⁶ Gather the people, sanctify the
        congregation,
    Assemble the elders,
    Gather the children and the
        nursing infants.
    Let the bridegroom come out of
        his room
    And the bride out of her bridal
        chamber.
[All people are to give themselves to seeking God without reservation. All normal
daily occupations are temporarily set
aside.]
¹⁷ Let the priests, the LORD's
    ministers,

*Weep between the porch and the
    altar,
And let them say, "Spare Thy
    people, O LORD,
And do not make Thine inheri-
    tance a reproach,
A byword among the nations.
Why should they among the
    peoples say,
'Where is their God?'"*

(Joel 2:15-17 NAS)

Here is God's promised response to the
prayer and fasting of His people:

23   *"So rejoice, O sons of Zion,
    And be glad in the LORD your
        God;
    For He has given you the early
        rain for your vindication.
    And He has poured down for you
        the rain,
    The early and latter rain as
        before.*
24   *And the threshing floors will be
        full of grain,
    And the vats will overflow with
        the new wine and oil.*

25   "Then I will make up to you for
          the years
      That the swarming locust has
          eaten,
      The creeping locust, the stripping
          locust, and the gnawing
          locust,
      My great army which I sent
          among you.
26   And you shall have plenty to eat
          and be satisfied,
      And praise the name of the LORD
          your God,
      Who has dealt wondrously with
          you;
      Then My people will never be put
          to shame.
27   Thus you will know that I am in
          the midst of Israel,
      And that I am the LORD your
          God
      And there is no other;
      And My people will never be put
          to shame.
28   And it will come about after this
      That I will pour out My Spirit on
          all mankind;
      And your sons and daughters
          will prophesy,

> Your old men will dream
>   dreams,
> Your young men will see visions.
> [29] And even on the male and female
>   servants
> I will pour out My Spirit in those
>   days."
>
> (Joel 2:23-29 NAS)

In response to prayer and fasting by His people, God says, "I will come to your help. I will change the whole situation, take away the dearth and the blight, and supply all your needs. There will be an abundance, an overflow, and no longer will you be a reproach among the nations. You will be able to lift up your heads, and other peoples will say, 'Look what God has done for them.'"

In particular, God promises that He will send His people the desperately needed former and latter rain. He then says, in a spiritual application of the rain, *"I will pour out My Spirit on all mankind."*

In the New Testament we read the words of the apostle Peter to the crowd that had assembled on the Day of Pentecost, after the Holy Spirit had come:

[16]*"But this is what was spoken of through the prophet Joel* [Peter links this to the prophecy of Joel cited above]:

[17]   *'AND IT SHALL BE IN THE LAST DAYS,' God says,*
    'THAT I WILL POUR FORTH OF MY SPIRIT UPON ALL MANKIND;
    AND YOUR SONS AND YOUR DAUGHTERS SHALL PROPHESY,
    AND YOUR YOUNG MEN SHALL SEE VISIONS,
    AND YOUR OLD MEN SHALL DREAM DREAMS;
[18]   *EVEN UPON MY BONDSLAVES, BOTH MEN AND WOMEN,*
    I WILL IN THOSE DAYS POUR FORTH OF MY SPIRIT
    AND THEY SHALL PROPHESY.' "
             (Acts 2:16-18 NAS)

God has prepared a worldwide outpouring of His Holy Spirit upon His church for these last days. It is God's answer to the desperate needs and pressures of this time. It is His answer for the satanic, ungodly forces that are coming against His people from so many areas, and to the blight and dearth in the church of God. God does not intend to leave His people helpless or at the mercy of all these evil pressures and forces. God has a provision. He has promised to pour out His Spirit and help His people on a supernatural level. However, He requires the condition be met that we seek Him with prayer and fasting, in a united and collective way.

Notice the promise in Joel 2:28: *"It will come about after this that I will pour out My Spirit on all mankind...."* After what? After we have met God's stated conditions. We are to consecrate a fast, call a solemn assembly, seek God, and come together with prayer and fasting. Then He says He will be faithful to His commitment to us. God says that He will come to you in the power and fullness of the Holy Spirit to change the whole situation. Instead of being fearful and defeated, you will become strong and effective. Instead of sneering at you, the world will stand back in awe and amazement when it sees how God has come to the help of His people.

In calling God's people to prayer and fasting, the message of Joel places a special responsibility upon the spiritual leaders of His people. Three classes of persons are singled out more than once for special mention. They are the priests, the ministers, and the elders. For instance, in Joel 1:13–14, we find: *"Gird yourselves with sackcloth, and lament, O priests; Wail, O ministers of the altar!...Proclaim a solemn assembly; gather the elders..."* Here the emphasis is on the priests, the ministers, and the elders.

In Joel 2:16–17, God instructions are: *"Gather the people, sanctify the congregation, assemble the elders... Let the priests, the LORD's ministers, weep between the porch and the altar...*" There is a desperate need for men of God in leadership who, by example, will show God's people this pattern of collective prayer and fasting to seek God's intervention on behalf of His people.

This applies to the nation in which we live. We need to see again the truth of that familiar verse in 2 Chronicles 7:14:

> [14]"...*if my people, who are called by my name, will humble themselves and pray and seek my face and turn from their wicked ways, then will I hear from heaven and will forgive their sin and will heal their land.*" (NIV)

I believe that is a message for us in these days. God is telling us once again He will intervene on a nationwide scale. He will not only show Himself strong on behalf of individuals and families, but on behalf of cities, communities, regions, and whole nations.

The kind of intervention God speaks about in 2 Chronicles 7:14 requires His people to meet His conditions. The first condition is, *"...if My people...will humble themselves."* We have seen in the course of our study that this means collective, united fasting and praying. From the Day of Atonement on, this has been the appointed way for God's people to humble themselves before Him, and God's ordinance has not changed. He is waiting for leaders who, in humility, will lead God's people in united prayer and fasting. Then He promises to hear, to forgive, and to heal the land.

Shaping History through Prayer and Fasting
Derek Prince

The times we are living in are scary, to say the least, yet what we are facing isn't new. History is replete with violent episodes of unimaginable carnage and terror. And what did people do about them? The only thing they could do—they prayed! Discover with Derek Prince how your prayers can make a difference. You can learn to touch the heart of God through effective fasting and prayer—prayer that will change the world!

———————————

ISBN: 978-0-88368-773-4 • Trade • 192 pages

www.whitakerhouse.com